Having grown up in the suburbs of Western Sydney and developing a fondness for all that is Australian. I have been delighted to be able to produce a childrens book that features the amazing and colourful features of the Australian Blue Wren.

I would like to thank my good friend Simon Creedy for his help with the design of my book.

Little Blue Wren Blue Wren.

Tonie Christian (TOPCAT) - Author

© 2025 COPYRIGHT BLACK CAT PUBLISHING

For *Natty* ...Always Shine

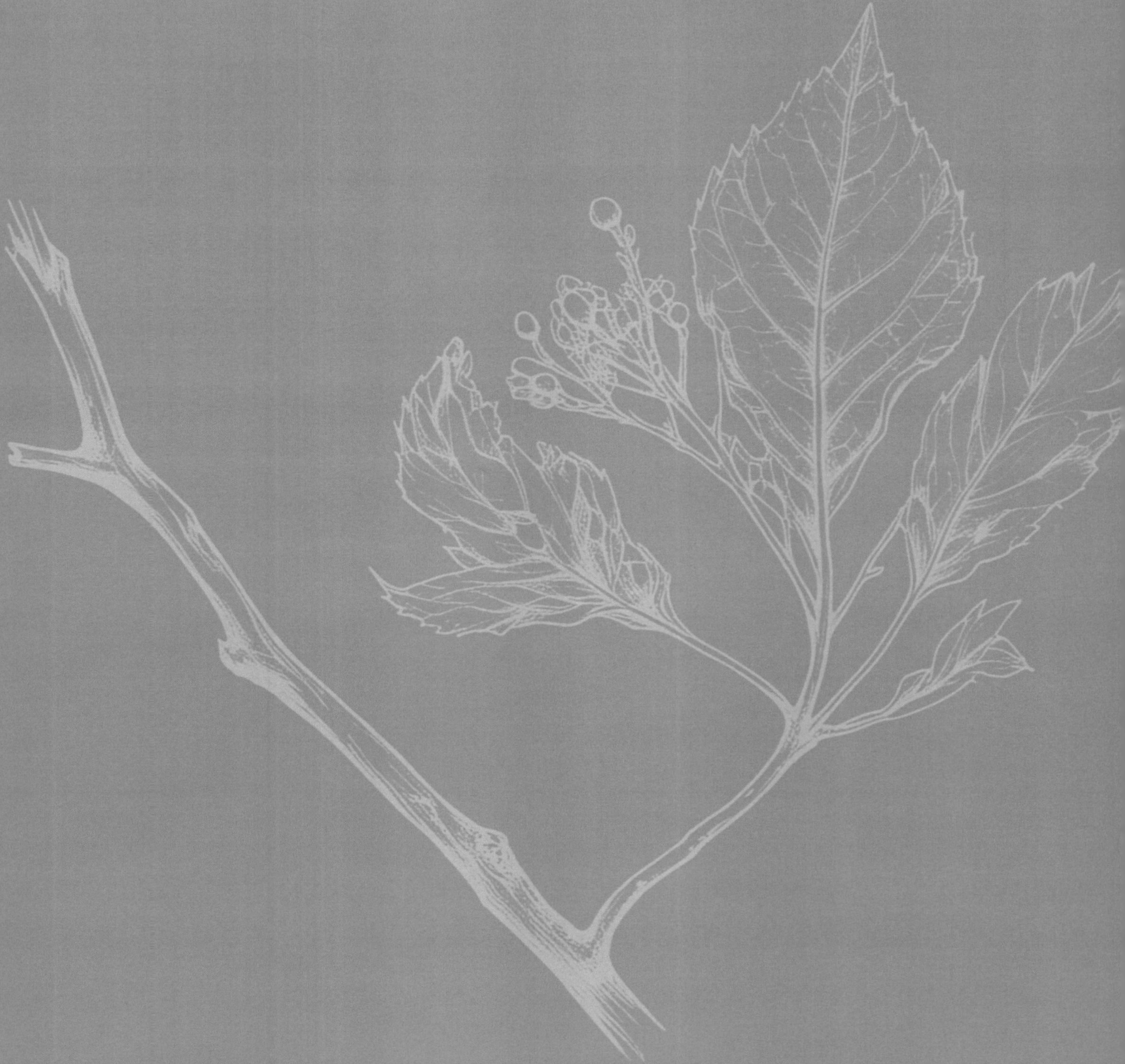

Little Blue Wren Blue Wren

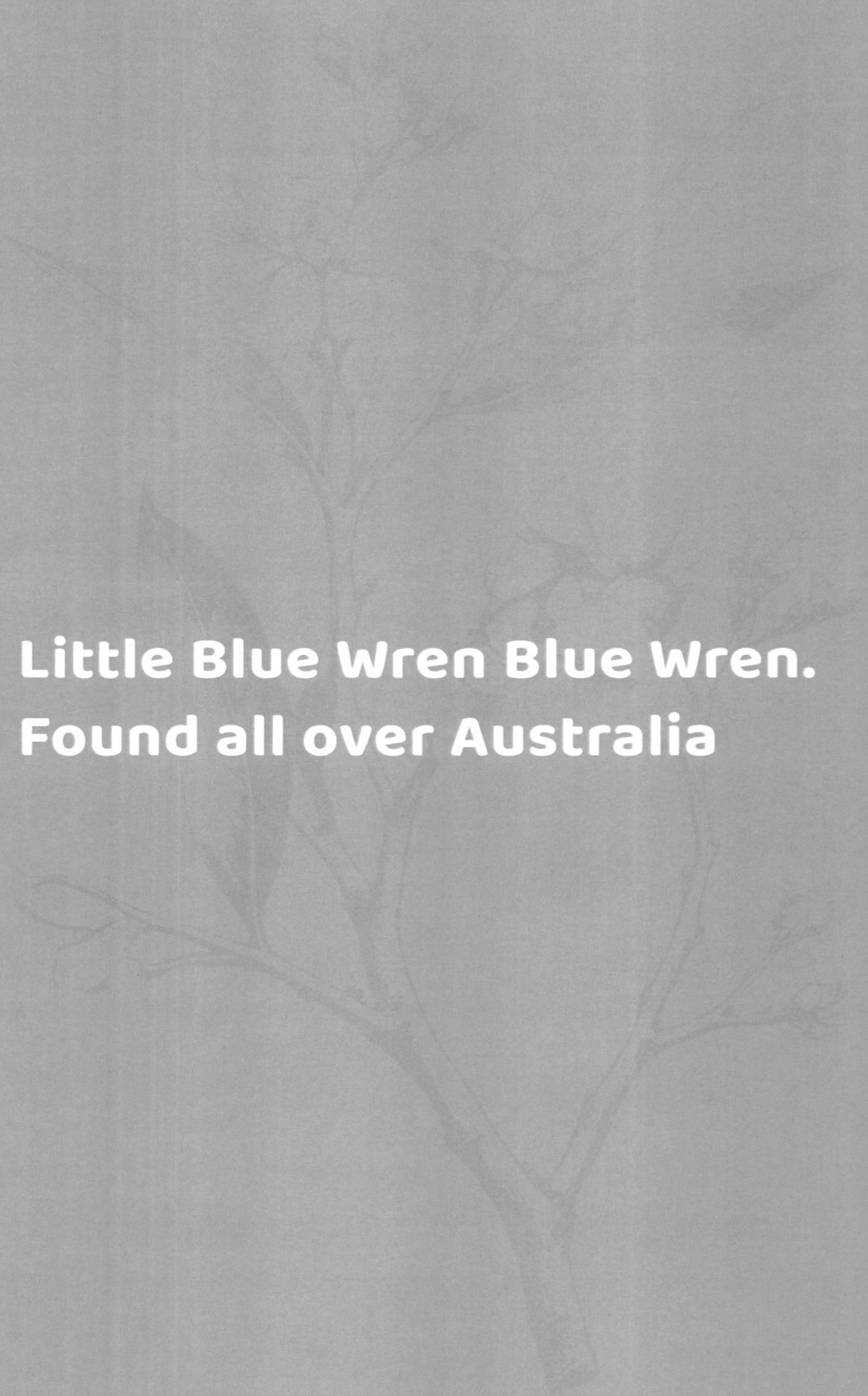

Little Blue Wren Blue Wren.
Found all over Australia

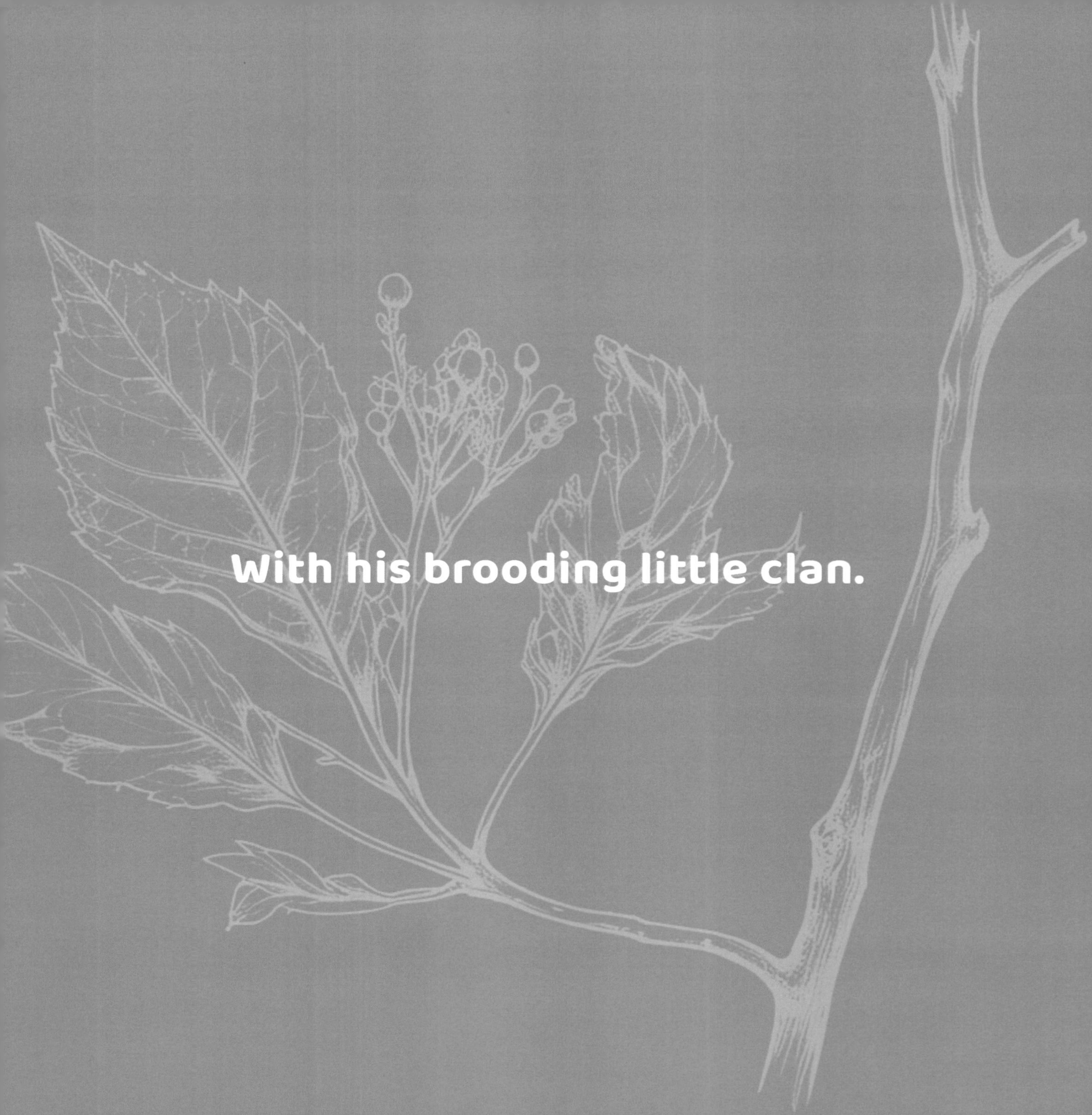

With his brooding little clan.

His nest in thickets

In closed razor barb,

Fenced with undulating maze

Of tunnel, vents and garb.

A little general

And day and night sentinel,

War painted blue black
And brown how sentimental.

Little inch high rotating
his wings.

A tiny helicopter that
loves to sing.

Not to long or distance flight,

But can live amongst thorns and bushland,

Near water and even on the mountain side.

With his hen they fly
side by side,

Carry a heavy shoulder
most times.

A little marauder whom
vents his charm,

And puffs and squeaks
underlying feats,

Foraging and stalking and
baulking little treats.

Boisterous and conniving on his tiny feathered little feet.

Oh little Blue Wren Blue Wren.
In meadows and thickets and
Where shadows blend.

Neighbourly in gardens

When the works done.

Its time to snuggle up
And huddle in the warm sun.

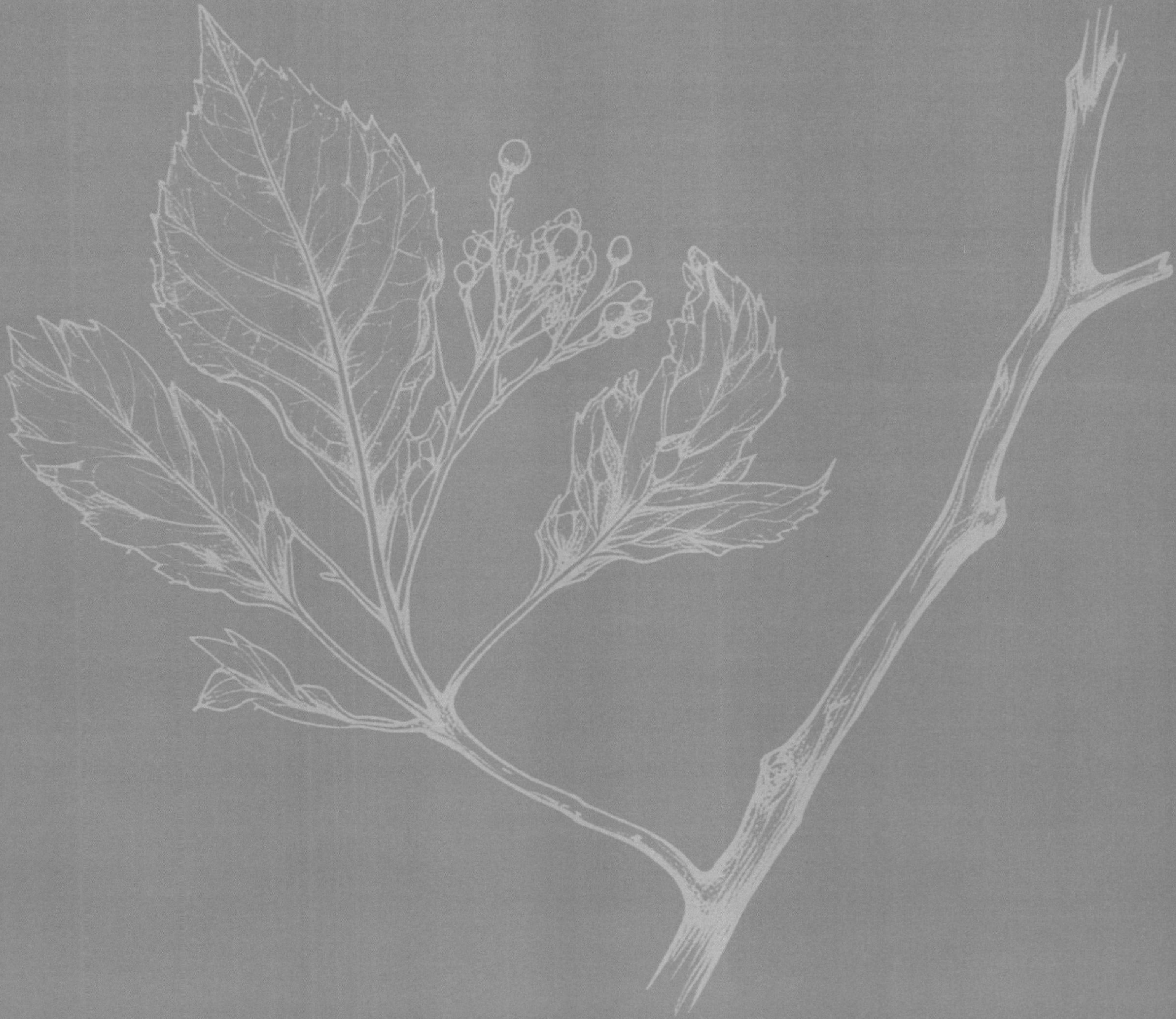

www.ingramcontent.com/pod product-compliance
Lightning Source LLC
Chambersburg PA
CBRC091536260326
41914CB00021B/1638